ANGEL BASKETS

A Little Story About The Shakers

by Mary Lyn Ray
Pictures by Jean Colquhoun

Martha Wetherbee Books
Sanbornton, New Hampshire

A leaf of love, for every child

I n 1842, when she was two years old, Cornelia French was brought to the Shakers at Mt. Lebanon, New York. Like many of the children the Shakers raised, Cornelia was possibly an orphan. She lived her life at Mt. Lebanon, and died there in 1914.

From the time she was sixteen, Cornelia helped to make baskets; for almost sixty years she was a basketmaker. Examples of her work may be seen at Winterthur Museum in Delaware, the Shaker Museum in New York and Fruitlands Museum in Massachusetts.

It was a cold country night. Cornelia had been left to live with the Shakers.

Under the stars the buildings looked like big boxes painted white: the way she imagined the homes of angels.

Far away the fields became hills and the hills became mountains and the mountains became sky.

Cornelia had been told this place was holy.

All the Shakers made one family. Old men and old women, young men and young women, little boys and little girls, they called each other "brother" and "sister." They all had one mother, who was Ann Lee, and one father, who was God. They lived in one big house and ate their meals in one big room.

Downstairs was a cellar and upstairs was an attic, and in between were the rooms where the Shakers slept.

On one side of a long straight hall were rooms where the men had their beds. On the other side were rooms for the boys. Down a different hall were rooms for the women and girls.

Cornelia liked the mystery of doors and drawers, and the cupboards built into the walls. She liked the stiff little chairs. And the stiff little bed, where she would sleep tonight and the next night and all the nights until she grew too big to fit it.

The big house seemed to hold her as if it loved her.

But sometimes in the dark a bad dream waked her, and then a sister came and sang to her.

Mother has come with her beautiful song, Ho Ho Tal La Me Ho.

She's come to bless her children dear, Ho Ho Tal La Me Ho, And

Christ your Savior will be near, Ho Ho Tal La Me Ho.

Cornelia was given a Shaker dress and Shaker shoes, and when she put them on, she looked like the other Shakers.

Days became weeks and weeks became months. Colors changed as seasons came and went. Yet here at the Shakers it seemed it was always Sunday.

There was a rule for everything. The Shakers called it "Order."

It was against order to ask for fancy hairbows. Or "to covet books with flourished pictures." Or "to have privacies in communication." It was even against order "to step with the left foot before the right foot."

Somedays Cornelia didn't like having rules. She walked with her left foot first. She whispered "privacies." And if she heard him at his chores, she giggled at a brother who sang funny, even though she knew it was against order to be unkind.

Abraham had been a singing master but now he was very old. His voice had become old too. And when he sang, some of the song "stuck in his throat, scratching and scrambling up long after the tune had ceased."

It made Cornelia laugh, unless someone caught her. Then she had to confess to the Eldress and promise to act better.

Twice a week Cornelia went to the meeting in the meetinghouse. There she learned songs the Shakers said that angels had sung to them, and learned dances made of squares and circles the angels had taught them to dance.

Sometimes in meeting everyone was given pretend gifts. Once Cornelia received a ball of love to bounce. Another time it was a little bell "to ring in union." Once it was a handkerchief, printed with her name and underneath "A Seal of Approbation," in the form of a little star.

Sometimes the family found leaves or hearts cut out of paper in their plates at breakfast. It was a secret where they came from, but they were meant to remind them to love God and be good children.

A B C D E F G H I J K L M

a b c d e f g h i j k l m n o p q r s

At the Shaker school Cornelia learned to add and multiply long numbers. She learned to read geographies with colored maps. And of course she learned to write the script all Shakers wrote.

NOPQRSTUVWXYZ

tuvwxyz& ☞ 1234567890.

Rose Hip Jam.

Take the fruit of the Sweetbriar wild rose or
Rosa Rubiginosa, wash hips, remove stiff
hairs, stems and calyx. Split open, remove
seeds. For each cup of fruit make a syrup of
1½ cups sugar and 1 cup water. Boil 4 min.,
add fruit and 2 tbbsp. lemon juice. Cover, boil
20 min. If fruit is not clear cook uncovered
until clear and thick.

When school was out, she practiced by copying recipes in the stone kitchen.

All the old men and the old women, the young men and young women, the littlest boys and the littlest girls helped with the work of the village.

They had many shops and mills and barns besides the big house they lived in.

When she was very young, Cornelia was taught to make her bed and to put the chairs in rows for meeting. When she was older, she learned to help at any job where extra hands were needed. Some days she measured flour and molasses in the kitchen. Some days she pasted labels on jars and bottles in the herb room.

Some jobs changed with the seasons. Cornelia always knew that spring was near when she was asked to help put away the winter blankets and lay them in the long drawers in the attic that smelled of lavender and roses.

One day Cornelia "put on the cap." This meant she was preparing to be a Shaker when she was old enough.

When she was fourteen, she left the children's order. When she was sixteen, she became a basketmaker.

In the fall the brothers who helped with the baskets put on their coats and went to the woods to look for black ash trees. Then they cut them and brought them back to the village. From some of the trees they peeled off long strips for splint. From others they cut small sticks from which they made rims and handles.

Then Daniel Boler who was the Elder in charge brought the new splint to the sisters.

The sisters took the splint and wove it around wooden molds to make the basket bodies. Then they put on rims and a handle. When they finished a basket, they took it and set it on a table to see if it would sit level.

At first Cornelia only laid up the bottoms. Then she learned to weave the sides and turn down the tops. Finally she learned to fit the rims and handle. Because her work was very good, she was also taught twilled patterns. The most difficult was "The Quadrifoil" but she practiced till she had it perfect. It had petals like a flower.

The brothers made baskets too. But theirs were usually meant for the barns and buildings in the village. Those the sisters made were for sale.

In one year the sisters made 4,000 baskets. Some were displayed in their shop. Others were shipped to stores across the country. The brothers packed them in great boxes and sent them on the train. Little girls Cornelia never knew learned to sew, keeping their scraps and needles in baskets she had made.

Sometimes Cornelia rode out in a wagon to deliver baskets in towns that were nearby. Other times she went on trips to mineral springs where the sisters sold their baskets in hotels when people from the cities came in the summer.

Then one day Cornelia signed the book and became a Shaker.

She could have left, but she chose to stay. She liked her Shaker home.

Every year when it was fall Cornelia and the sisters began making baskets.
All winter they made baskets. Then when spring came they stopped. Some of
them sorted seeds for the garden. Some of them sewed cloaks. Some of them
made shirts for the brothers. Some made jam and pickles. Then fall came again,
and again they began making baskets.

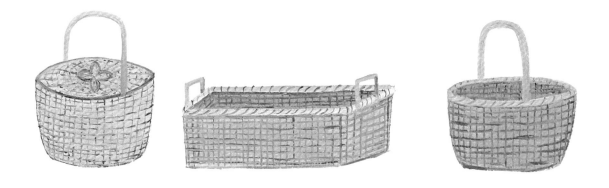

By the time Cornelia was an old woman, she had helped to make 71,244 baskets. And all of these were beautiful and light and filled with love. Because that was how the Shakers made things.

When she was so old she died, Cornelia's spirit went to the spirit world.
And there, like the sandman who scatters dreams,
she was given a basket
to scatter love.